MODERN ERAS
the mid
1980s
to the early
1990s
UNCOVERED

KU-252-054

# From Compact Discs
# to the Gulf War

TURRIFF ACADEMY
LIBRARY

Pat Levy and Sean Sheehan

Raintree

**www.raintreepublishers.co.uk**
Visit our website to find out more information about **Raintree** books.

To order:
☎ Phone 44 (0) 1865 888113
📄 Send a fax to 44 (0) 1865 314091
💻 Visit the Raintree Bookshop at **www.raintreepublishers.co.uk** to browse our catalogue and order online.

First published in Great Britain by Raintree, Halley Court, Jordan Hill, Oxford, OX2 8EJ, part of Harcourt Education.
Raintree is a registered trademark of Harcourt Education Ltd.

© Harcourt Education Ltd 2006
The moral right of the proprietor has been asserted.

All rights reserved. No part of this publication may be reproduced, stored in a retrieval system, or transmitted in any form or by any means, electronic, mechanical, photocopying, recording, or otherwise, without either the prior written permission of the publishers or a licence permitting restricted copying in the United Kingdom issued by the Copyright Licensing Agency Ltd, 90 Tottenham Court Road, London W1T 4LP (www.cla.co.uk).

Editorial: Melanie Copland and Lucy Beevor
Design: Michelle Lisseter and
Bridge Creative Services Ltd
Picture Research: Mica Brancic and Ginny Stroud-Lewis
Production: Duncan Gilbert

Originated by Chroma Graphics (Overseas) Pte. Ltd
Printed and bound in China by South China Printing Company

ISBN 1 844 43957 7
10 09 08 07 06
10 9 8 7 6 5 4 3 2 1

British Library Cataloguing in Publication Data
Sheehan, Sean
From Compact Discs to the Gulf War. – (Modern Eras Uncovered)
909.8'28

A full catalogue record for this book is available from the British Library.

Acknowledgements
Allstar Picture Library p. 4; Associated Press pp. 15, 35, 39; Corbis p. 23; Corbis/ Alan Schein Photography p. 10; Corbis/Alain Nogues p. 26; Corbis/Bernard Bisson p. 13; Corbis/Bettmann pp. 16 (both), 31; Corbis/Bureau L.A. Collection p. 45; Corbis/Gideon Mendel p. 38; Corbis/Jacques Langevin p. 30; Corbis/Jacques M. Chenet p. 11; Corbis/Lynn Goldsmith p. 7; Corbis/Natalie Fobes p. 17; Corbis/Owen Franken p. 27; Corbis/Peter Turnley pp. 5, 18, 42, 43; Corbis/Reuters p. 22; Corbis/Sgyma/ Bernard Bisson p. 28; Corbis/Sygma/ Lu-Hovasse Diane p. 36; Corbis/Sygma/Alain Nogues p. 12; Corbis/Sygma/Langevin Jacques p. 47; Corbis/Sygma/Patrick Robert p. 44; Getty Images p. 14; Getty Images/Hulton Archive p. 20; Getty Images/Time Life Pictures pp. 21, 25, 34; Rex Features pp. 33, 40; The Advertising Archives Ltd pp. 6, 8, 49; The Kobal Collection/Orion/Ken Regan p. 21; Topfoto p. 19; Topfoto/Associated Press p. 29; Topfoto/ImageWorks p. 32.

Cover photograph (top) reproduced with permission of Corbis Sygma, and photograph (bottom) reproduced with permission of Getty Images/Time Life Pictures, Allen Tannenbaum.

Every effort has been made to contact copyright holders of any material reproduced in this book. Any omissions will be rectified in subsequent printings if notice is given to the publishers.

| ABERDEENSHIRE LIBRARY AND INFORMATION SERVICE | |
|---|---|
| 1665685 | |
| CAW | 333611 |
| J909.828 | £12.50 |
| | PORP |

Aberdeenshire Library and Information Service
www.aberdeenshire.gov.uk/libraries
Renewals Hotline 01224 661511        909.828

– 8 SEP 2009

ABERDEENSHIRE
LIBRARIES

WITHDRAWN
FROM LIBRARY

LEVY, Patricia

From compact discs to the
Gulf War

ABERDEENSHIRE
LIBRARIES

WITHDRAWN
FROM LIBRARY

ABERDEENSHIRE LIBRARIES

ABS 2005548

# CONTENTS

Any words appearing in the text in bold, **like this**, are explained in the glossary.

# REWRITING HISTORY

The mid 1980s was a fairly quiet time in politics. Ronald Reagan had been re-elected president of the United States and Margaret Thatcher was re-elected as prime minister of the UK. They shared a view of the world that was based upon the **Cold War**. This was the state of hostility between the **West** and the **USSR** that had existed for 40 years. The West felt they stood for freedom while the USSR was, in Reagan's words, "an evil empire."

People who did not share these views claimed that Reagan and Thatcher had created a selfish world, where freedom meant the rich became richer and the poor stayed poor. To others, though, the 1980s was a time when people could make something of their lives, develop their talents, and enjoy their success. There was a mood of confidence and prosperity. Designer labels became important and the term "power dressing" described a type of fashion for women especially, but also for men. Music and dance fashions were loud and brash, and young people had the money to buy new electronic goods such as compact disc players. A new cartoon show, *The Simpsons*, was about a middle-class US family that was often very selfish but also very likeable.

The cartoon series *The Simpsons* became popular with people of all ages. The first episode was shown in December 1989.

The world was also changing in ways that many people did not notice at the time. In countries where **Islam** was the main religion there was a growing sense of confidence. Some Islamic leaders called for a return to what they called the fundamental (basic) values of Islam. These **fundamentalists** began to appeal to **Muslims** who felt their people and culture were under threat from the West.

Big changes were also taking place in the USSR. The new Soviet leader, Mikhail Gorbachev, knew that his country's **economy** was in serious trouble. He began to make changes that led to a new map for parts of the world. An age that began with the compact disc ended with the end of the Cold War. It was not the end of war everywhere, however, as a new conflict developed in the **Middle East** when the first Gulf War occurred.

A Palestinian man pleads with an Israeli soldier for the release of his son from Am' Aricamp, Ram Allah, West Bank, in 1988.

## Different economies

This bar chart shows the annual rate of development for the economies of different regions of the world, between the mid 1970s and the early 1990s. By comparing them it can be seen what parts of the world were progressing and what parts were not.

A graph showing the economic growth of different regions between the mid 1970s and the early 1990s.

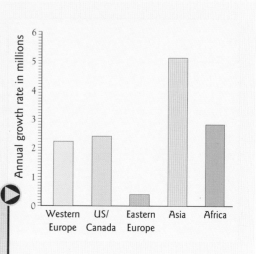

Annual growth rate in millions

Western Europe | US/ Canada | Eastern Europe | Asia | Africa

In the south of England in the mid 1980s people were quite wealthy, the majority were white and many lived in **suburbs**. In southern inner-city areas, and in the towns and cities of northern England all was not so well. There were areas of **urban decay** and poor neighbourhoods. Many teenagers listened to rap music and danced to house, garage, or techno music in clubs. The average teenager had a personal stereo, vinyl records (LPs) for a stereo system, and perhaps a television in their bedroom.

## Fashion and music

In 1985, padded shoulders and **masculine** suits – popular since the early 1980s – still dominated women's fashion. Aerobics, jogging, and gym sessions had become popular with **middle-class** women and this sparked off fashions in fitness clothing. **Lycra** leotards, trainers, and tracksuits – complete with designer logos – became fashionable.

By the end of the 1980s, fashion began to look back to earlier periods in history for its inspiration. Designers came up with 1950s-style baseball zipper jackets and mixing miniskirts from the 1960s with fitted blouses from the 1950s. For men, the very narrow "skinny ties" that were popular in the 1950s and 1960s were in style again. At the same time, older bands such as The Rolling Stones, The Who, and The Beach Boys produced popular records during this time, and toured countries with live performances.

A fashion advertisement, from the 1980s, shows the square padded shoulders typical of women's clothing around this time.

# Hip-Hop

In the 1970s in New York, United States, a new form of music developed, called Hip-Hop. It was based around the music of some New York clubs where the DJs stopped the lyrics and extended the drumming track, while talking over the drumbeat to encourage people to dance, and calling out to friends. This eventually led to "MCs" (Master of Ceremonies) rhyming to the beats. This soon became known as rapping.

By 1985 Hip-Hop, or rap music, had become popular all over the United States and around the world. Public Enemy, RUN-DMC, LL Cool J, and others performed raps that were about society for example, describing the experiences of African-American inner-city teenagers. A less positive side of rap was "gangsta rap," which used lyrics to describe the underworld of drug dealing and gang warfare. Rappers usually wore lots of gold and loose, baggy jeans or dungarees. Some rappers, such as De La Soul, stressed that you did not have to wear gold and expensive shoes to be cool. It was more important to be original.

The rap group RUN-DMC pose in baggy trousers and gold chains in 1987. They were the first ever rappers to become huge stars.

## Rap talk

Rap has its own language, which changes almost as rapidly as the music. Here are some rap terms that started being used in the 1980s:

bail – leave
boyz – friends
chillin' – relaxing
crib – place of residence
crew – good friends
diss – disrespect
fly – appealing
homie, homey, homeboy – friend
hood – neighbourhood

kickin' – appealing, or just hanging out ("we're just kickin' it.")
my bad – my mistake
phat – very cool
sitch – situation
sup – what's up
tight – attractive
wack – stupid, dumb, not to one's liking

# The compact disc

By 1985, digital technology had become a part of everyday life in the West. The technology behind compact discs (CDs) had been invented in the 1960s. In the 1970s, the technology was put to use by television companies that wanted to record programmes. By the late 1970s, the technology had moved on, and was now cheap enough to sell to the public. By the early 1980s, the first music CD players and discs were being sold. In 1984, Sony invented a portable CD music player. CDs had many advantages over the old vinyl records and cassette tapes:

- much better quality sound
- longer lasting
- less easily scratched
- able to store much more music.

By 1985, CD players were well on their way to becoming an essential leisure item for both teenagers and their parents. By 1986, 3 million CD players and 53 million music CDs had been sold in the United States. CD players for cars had also been developed. By 1987, video CDs had been developed and by 1988, the technology was in place for recordable CDs, although these did not become available for another few years. In the United States, by the end of the 1980s, 9 million CD players were being sold each year.

Compact disc players, such as this one shown, were widely available from the mid 1980s.

# Computers and CDs

From the mid 1980s onwards, personal computers (PCs) were starting to become common household items. Using an operating system called Windows, computer users could call up the programs they wanted from a series of icons on the monitor. Apple computers had already produced a similar operating system called the Macintosh machine. The small numbers of people who could afford it bought one or other of these two computer systems. In 1985, CD technology was adapted to computers, making them capable of loading more complex programs. The use of CDs and increasing memory sizes of PCs made computer technology more and more a part of everyday life.

## How CDs work

CDs use digital technology. Information, such as music or pictures, is translated into a code based on the numbers 1 and 0. Known as a **binary code**, this system of holding information can be represented electronically by a pulse of electricity (the 1) or by the absence of a pulse of electricity (the 0). CD technology copies these 1s and 0s on to a thin layer of aluminium (2 in the diagram), covered in a plastic layer (3) for protection. If you look at a CD under a microscope you will see one of the layers is marked with tiny pits (4). A laser in the CD player passes over the pits as the CD spins and a computer programme in the CD player reads these as music, pictures, or whatever information is recorded on the CD.

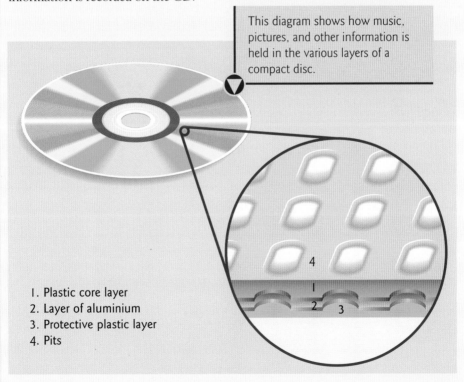

This diagram shows how music, pictures, and other information is held in the various layers of a compact disc.

1. Plastic core layer
2. Layer of aluminium
3. Protective plastic layer
4. Pits

# New forms of art and entertainment

Many ordinary people made a lot of money in the 1980s in various different businesses. People's spending power was a sign of their success in life. Buying rare paintings by great artists became a way of investing money. A famous painting would increase in value every year. Two paintings by Dutch painter Vincent van Gogh, auctioned in the 1980s, fetched record prices of US$39 million and US$53 million.

## Architecture

The style of new buildings reflected the confidence and wealth of the West. In Paris, in 1981, the architect I. M. Pei designed an extension to the Louvre art gallery. It was very modern, in the shape of a pyramid and covered with glass. In 1986, the same architect built the Javits Convention Center in New York, United States. Also covered in glass, and occupying five city blocks, it was a huge construction. The interior of the building was supported by pillars, which looked like champagne glasses. New York's 68-storey Trump Building, with a bronze glass exterior, showed the wealth of its multi-millionaire owner, Donald Trump. In London's run-down docklands area a huge complex called Canary Wharf was built and became an important business centre.

The spectacular Javits Convention Center in Manhattan, New York, was designed by I. M. Pei in 1986.

## The Simpsons and Seinfeld

In 1986, a 5-minute cartoon section was shown on Tracy Ullman's comedy show in the United States. It featured a family of two parents, a son, and two daughters. By 1989, *The Simpsons* was its own show and it seemed to reflect what was unpleasant as well as what was loveable about middle-class ordinary families at the end of the 20th century. The Simpson children, like their father Homer, did not always behave properly; they also ate unhealthy food and spent too much time watching television. At the same time, the family tried to help one another survive in a world of bullying students, unfair bosses, and poor wages. Audiences recognized this world and could relate to the show. It became the longest running sitcom in history and is still going strong. In the United States, in 1990, a more adult comedy series called *Seinfeld* was first shown. It also featured characters that were often selfish and self-centred, coping humorously with everyday situations.

### Live Aid

In July 1985, the biggest rock concert ever organized was held on two continents, linked by satellite, and broadcast around the world. In aid of **famine** relief in Ethiopia, the concert included performances by famous names such as The Rolling Stones, The Beach Boys, David Bowie, Tina Turner, Madonna, Led Zeppelin, Bob Dylan, The Who, and Queen, who all performed for free. The show ended with groups of performers on stage, singing "Do They Know It's Christmas?" in the UK and "We Are the World" in the United States. The concert raised over £150 million (US$245 million) to help people dying of starvation. The money came from millions of people who phoned in to make donations.

This was the huge Live Aid concert stage in Philadelphia, Pennsylvania, United States. Thousands of spectators gathered to watch the charity rock concert on 13 July, 1985.

# DEATH AND DISASTER

For people in the UK, the mid 1980s seemed hopeful. It looked possible that the violence that had surrounded the question of independence in Northern Ireland for fifteen years might soon end. The Anglo-Irish Agreement was signed between the Irish and the UK governments and it seemed as if a peaceful solution might be possible. Unfortunately, this did not happen and the violence continued.

## Attacking planes and airports

On 14 June 1985, members of a group calling itself Islamic Jihad hijacked a TWA flight from Athens to Rome. They demanded the release of 700 Arab men being held prisoner in Israel, in exchange for the release of the hostages. For two weeks the hijackers forced the pilots to fly the plane between Beirut and Algeria, and they negotiated with officials from Israel when the plane was not in the air. One United States passenger was killed and his body thrown out on to the runway tarmac as a warning. The rest of the passengers, except 39 Americans, were released. At the end of June these 39 hostages were released on 30 June. The 700 prisoners were released by Israel over the next few weeks, and the hijackers escaped.

## Air India

Ten days after the TWA hijacking, an Air India 747 flying from Toronto to London exploded over the west coast of Ireland, killing all 329 people on board. It was not known at the time, but the bomb was put on the plane by **Sikh extremists**, made angry by the Indian government's attack on the Sikh temple at Amritsar the year before. They were also responsible for what had happened less than an hour earlier, when another bomb exploded at Tokyo airport in a piece of luggage about to be put into another Air India flight.

## The Lockerbie disaster

On 21 December 1988, Pan Am Flight 103 exploded 10 kilometres (6 miles) above the Scottish town of Lockerbie during it's flight from Frankfurt, Germany, to New York, United States. All 259 people onboard died, and 11 people were killed by the falling wreckage. It was an act of international terrorism on a huge scale. Global police investigations led eventually to 49-year-old Libyan Abdelbaset Ali Mohmed al Megrahi. He was prosecuted and imprisoned for life in January 2001.

Masked Islamic Jihad terrorists guard the airplane door during the hijacking of the TWA flight from Athens to Rome, 29 June 1985.

## The *Achille Lauro*

In October of 1985, a **PLO** group hijacked a cruise ship, the *Achille Lauro*, in the Mediterranean and made it sail to Egypt. They wanted Israel to release Palestinian prisoners. One of the 454 passengers, a Jewish man, was shot and his body thrown overboard. There was a **stalemate** for a few days until the Egyptian government, who the PLO had agreed to talk to, offered the hijackers safe passage out of the country if they surrendered. They left the ship and boarded a plane out of Egypt, but US jet fighter planes forced it to land in Sicily. The Italian government arrested the terrorists, and four of them were tried and sentenced to long prison terms. Abu Abbas, the alleged mastermind of the attack, fled jail and was arrested in April 2003. He died in custody in 2004.

Some of the hostages on the *Achille Lauro* cruise ship are taken ashore at Port Said, Egypt, after the PLO hijackers surrender, on 10 October 1985.

# The *Rainbow Warrior*

Many people were concerned about nuclear weapons tests that were being done by France, the UK, the United States, and the USSR. They were testing their nuclear weapons in remote locations or underground and many people worried what the long-term consequences of this might be. In 1971, an organization was formed to protest against United States nuclear testing at Amchitka Island in Alaska. The organization sent a boat out to the testing site and drew world attention to what was happening there. This group of Canadian protestors eventually became Greenpeace, a worldwide organization that by 1985 had hundreds of thousands of members.

## French nuclear testing

French scientists tested nuclear weapons on Moruroa Atoll, a remote island in the Pacific Ocean. In the early 1970s Greenpeace ships attempted to sail to Moruroa and tried to stop the tests taking place. However, one of their ships was rammed and damaged by the French Navy boats surrounding the area. This incident drew the world's attention to French nuclear testing and, in 1974, France announced that in future its nuclear tests would take place underground.

## The *Rainbow Warrior*

The *Rainbow Warrior* was the flagship of Greenpeace. In 1985, with underground French nuclear testing due in the Pacific, it sailed to New Zealand with the intention of leading a **flotilla** of ships into the testing zone. On 10 July, French government agents planted two bombs on the *Rainbow Warrior* as it lay in harbour in Auckland. The bombs exploded, sinking the ship and killing one of its crew. Two days later the New Zealand police arrested two of the bombers, who had been operating under the orders of the French government.

The bombed Greenpeace ship the *Rainbow Warrior* sinks off the coast of Auckland, New Zealand, on 10 July 1985.

## The French admit their involvement

At first the French government denied all connection to the attack but later admitted it was involved. The French defence minister resigned and the head of the secret service lost his job. The bombers were eventually tried and went to prison, each sentenced to ten years for manslaughter. Six other members of the French team escaped prosecution. Even though the French government had admitted its involvement, it demanded that the bombers be released into French custody. When this was denied the French government threatened to ban New Zealand from exporting goods to France (see November 1991 in the timeline below).

### Consequences of the *Rainbow Warrior* bombing:

**June 1986**: the **United Nations** Secretary General agrees to act as a go-between for the French and New Zealand governments

**July 1986**: France pays the New Zealand government US$13 million in compensation for what they did on New Zealand territory. The two bombers are released by New Zealand to spend three years confined to a French island, Hao in French Polynesia.

**December 1987**: one of the bombers is allowed back to France because of illness

**1987**: the French government pays US$8.16 million in compensation to Greenpeace

**May 1988**: the second bomber is released back to France

**November 1991**: a third bomber is arrested in Switzerland, but the New Zealand government does not take this further because of French threats of further **sanctions** on exporting their goods to France.

French Army Major, Alain Marfart, is arrested for his involvement in the bombing of the *Rainbow Warrior*. He was sentenced to ten years in prison, but was later allowed back to France because of illness.

# More bad news

## *Challenger*

In 1986, the United States was celebrating the twenty-fifth anniversary of manned space flight. The space programme was now all about the space shuttle and its various missions. In 1986, fifteen flights were planned, but the first of them, in January 1986, was very much in the public eye. This was because one of the crew members was actually a **civilian** schoolteacher called Christa McAuliffe. After being postponed several times because of technical difficulties and weather problems, the shuttle, with a total crew of seven, finally launched. However, ground crews spotted smoke and then flames trailing from the machine, and just 73 seconds after take-off *Challenger* exploded.

*Challenger* crew members leave for the shuttle launchpad at Kennedy Space Center, Florida, United States. 73 seconds after liftoff, the shuttle exploded, killing the entire crew.

An immediate investigation was ordered. This showed that a tiny rubber ring had failed to seal a joint, allowing hot gases to escape and catch fire. The investigation also criticised the National Aeronautics and Space Administration (NASA) for allowing the mission to go ahead despite engineers' worries that it might not be ready. The space programme was suspended. The tragedy came as a severe blow to US national pride and made many people question the value of the space programme. However, several technical modifications were made to the design of the shuttle and the space programme resumed in 1988 with the new shuttle, *Discovery*.

## Northern Ireland

In Northern Ireland, talks were taking place between the Irish and UK governments. There was still no solution, however, to the conflict between those who wanted Northern Ireland to remain part of the UK and those who wanted it to be united with the rest of Ireland. Northern Ireland became a society divided between **Protestant loyalists** and **Unionists** who wanted to remain a part of the UK, and **Catholic nationalists** and **Republicans** who felt that they were treated like second-class citizens and who wanted Northern Ireland united with the rest of Ireland. Since the 1970s, this conflict had become an increasingly violent one. Both sides used violence and civilians were often the victims.

In 1987, the Irish Republican Army (**IRA**) planted a bomb in the small town of Enniskillen in Northern Ireland. It exploded as a Second World War Remembrance Day service was taking place. The explosion killed 11 people and injured 63.

In 1988, three IRA members were shot and killed in Gibraltar by an army team from the UK. The IRA members were unarmed at the time and the UK government was accused of a "shoot to kill" policy.

## More disasters

In December 1985, armed terrorists attacked two ticket desks belonging to the Israeli airline El Al in both Rome and Vienna airports. Fifteen people died and many more were injured. In December 1988, in Armenia, part of the USSR, an earthquake destroyed three towns. It killed between 40,000 and 100,000 people and left hundreds of thousands homeless. In March 1989, the *Exxon Valdez* oil tanker split apart off the coast of Alaska, releasing thousands of tons of oil into the sea. In October 1989, an earthquake in San Francisco killed 63 people.

Volunteers spray clean water on to the oil-covered rocks of an Alaskan island, after the *Exxon Valdez* oil spill, March 1989.

# Chernobyl

In April 1986, scientists in Scandinavia detected unusually high levels of **radiation** being carried on the wind from the direction of the USSR. A few days later, Soviet officials announced that there had been a minor accident at the Chernobyl nuclear power station in the Ukraine. However, the clouds of **radioactive** material were increasing and spreading across Europe, reaching the UK in the west and Greece in the south. News began to emerge that thousands of people were being **evacuated** from Kiev, a city near Chernobyl. The Soviet government then asked for international help to put out a fire at the power station. A US spy satellite took pictures of it, showing major devastation. Finally, after almost three weeks, the USSR admitted what had happened.

In a May 1986 television broadcast, the Soviet leader Mikhail Gorbachev finally admits that a massive explosion had taken place at the Chernobyl nuclear power station.

## Wildlife after the Chernobyl explosion

In the years since the evacuation around Chernobyl, the area has changed dramatically. With no humans living there, plant life has taken over. However, many of the plants in the wooded areas around Chernobyl have **mutated** as a result of the radiation. People that have visited the area talk of a forest of wonders where plants look strange and in some cases have grown huge. Some animals have survived in the area although it seems that some bird life has suffered permanent **genetic** damage.

## A nuclear explosion

At the power station an experiment had been taking place to see how long a **nuclear reactor** could go on producing electricity after it had been shut down. The people doing the experiment ignored, or forgot, several safety procedures and the reactor overheated, causing an explosion. The explosion blew off the roof of the building and a plume of radioactive material was thrown into the air. As fires continued to burn fire fighters moved into the area, but many of them died very quickly from radiation poisoning. Eventually the fires were brought under control and, although cement was poured over the reactor to smother it and contain the radioactive material inside, the area still remains unsafe.

## The world's reaction

Suddenly Europe had to cope with huge clouds of radioactive gases over its cities and countryside. The explosion released more radioactive material than every other nuclear explosion and test that had taken place since nuclear power had been invented. The immediate area around Chernobyl became far too dangerous for humans to live in. Finland and Sweden were badly hit because the wind had carried the radioactive material northwards. It looked as if deaths from cancer would increase over the following decades. In order to avoid panic, some governments, including the UK and France, tried to play down the amount of nuclear radiation that was in the atmosphere.

When nuclear power stations had first been opened they had been greeted as wonders of science. They produced cheap, clean energy. Suddenly, the world saw what might happen if things went wrong. Many people came to the opinion that the risks of nuclear power outweighed the benefits.

This severely deformed piglet, born two years after the Chernobyl disaster, shows the dangerous after-effects of radioactive material.

# THE END OF THE COLD WAR

The distrust between the USSR and the United States, the Cold War, was based on two very different ideas about how best to organize society. **Capitalism**, the economic system of the West and promoted by the United States, is based on the private ownership of industry. Under the **communist** system in the USSR, industry was owned and controlled by the government. Thatcher, the UK prime minister, believed firmly in capitalism and strongly supported the United States. For this reason, permission was gladly given for US nuclear weapons to be stored at military bases in the UK. At one of these, at the US Air Force Base at Greenham Common in England, a women's peace camp was established and regular protests took place.

## Gorbachev and the Soviet Union

Gorbachev was elected leader of the USSR (Union of Soviet Socialist Republics) in 1985. He was determined to improve life for the people of the fifteen republics of the USSR. Russia was the largest republic and made up about half of the total population of the USSR. Russia was also the most powerful republic because of its military strength, and no other Soviet republic could challenge its leadership of the USSR. Russia kept a tight control over the lives of everyone and the lack of **democracy** made people afraid to criticise the system.

Mikhail Gorbachev talks to the citizens of Sofia, Bulgaria, after his election as leader of the USSR in March 1985.

## Perestroika

Gorbachev was a communist, but he knew the Soviet system was failing to give its citizens a good standard of living. He introduced policies known as **perestroika**, a word meaning "changing the structure of something." Gorbachev set about relaxing the tight control of the government over the economy. Before perestroika people had little say over the kind of work they did, and the economic system was slow and inefficient. Perestroika allowed small businesses to be set up that were not controlled by the government. The power that the government had over factories and other places of work was also reduced.

## Glasnost

Gorbachev realized that the government also had too much control over people's lives. He wanted a freer society so that new ideas could be put to use and people's different talents could be used to improve life for everyone. His changes were called **glasnost**, meaning "openness" and the opposite of "silence" or "forbidden." Because of glasnost, many artists, writers, and film-makers whose work was once banned were now allowed to express themselves.

A member of the Russian Socialist Movement for Perestroika holds up a comical caricature of President Landbergis of Lithuania in an effort to establish perestroika in that communist country.

## What made a Russian laugh?

A joke from the days before Gorbachev introduced democratic reforms:

"A worker is watching television and can only find channels showing a long and boring speech by a Soviet politician. He twiddles with the television knob until finally he discovers a channel without a picture of the politician, but up pops a member of the KGB [the government security force] in his uniform. He is wagging his finger and saying, 'What are you doing? Stop doing that!'"

# Ending the Cold War

The Cold War never developed into actual fighting between the United States and the USSR – this would have been a "hot war." They fought in another way, by supporting and arming opposite sides in wars involving other countries. Many wars in foreign countries were kept going only because they were supported by one or both sides in the Cold War. Most of the major wars fought around the world after the Second World War were related to the Cold War in this way. These wars killed millions of people in Central and South America, Africa, the Middle East, and in central and south-east Asia.

Gorbachev realized that the Cold War was stopping living standards from rising in the USSR. Huge amounts of money were being spent developing, building, and maintaining nuclear weapons in an attempt to keep up with the United States. Gorbachev wanted to use this money to improve the Soviet economy and so he set about ending the Cold War.

The world was taken by surprise when Gorbachev announced in 1986 that all nuclear weapons should be eliminated around the world. To start with, he suggested removing all medium-range nuclear missiles from Europe. The following year he announced that Soviet forces would be withdrawn from Afghanistan, a country where a "hot war" was kept going by the Cold War.

A group of happy Soviet soldiers wave from the top of a tank as they begin the withdrawal from Afghanistan, 15 May 1988.

Gorbachev and President Reagan of the United States met to discuss and agree on the removal of nuclear weapons from Europe. After a three-day summit, in 1987, both leaders signed the Intermediate-range Nuclear Forces Treaty, which was the first attempt to reverse the nuclear arms race. The world realized just how serious Gorbachev was when he declared to the United Nations in 1988 that the Soviet army would be reduced by half a million men. He went on to say, "Force, or the threat of force, can not and should not be instruments of foreign policy." This was an astonishing announcement. The Cold War depended on the military strength of both sides and here was the leader of one of those sides virtually withdrawing from the contest. Gorbachev was bringing about the end of the Cold War.

Soviet leader Mikhail Gorbachev and US President Ronald Reagan sign the Intermediate Range Nuclear Forces (INF) Treaty, virtually signalling the end of the Cold War, on 8 December 1987.

## A Cold War dictionary

**cruise missile**: missile that flies for a long distance, powered by an engine, and fired from an aircraft, the ground, a ship, or submarine

**first strike**: first move in a conflict. In nuclear warfare, the first strike is an attempt to destroy the enemy's ability to strike back with its own nuclear weapons.

**MAD**: Mutually Assured Destruction, meaning both sides having an equal ability to destroy one another

**NATO**: countries of the North Atlantic Treaty Organization **allied** to the United States in the Cold War

**Warsaw Pact**: a treaty creating a defence organization for countries allied to the USSR

# Eastern Europe demands change

Gorbachev had declared that it was important for countries to have the freedom to choose their own form of government. This was far from the days of the Cold War when the USSR, in order to feel secure, had kept Eastern European governments under its control. In the past, two of these countries, Hungary and Czechoslovakia, had been invaded by Soviet troops when they refused to do what the USSR wanted. Now, however, everything was different. The Cold War was coming to an end and Soviet troops had been withdrawn from Eastern Europe.

## Taking the lid off

Gorbachev encouraged the communist governments of Eastern Europe to reform by introducing their own policies of perestroika. Gorbachev wanted them to reform so that they would stop depending on money from the USSR. Hungary made a start in 1988. The leader of its communist government was removed from power and a more open government was formed. By taking the lid off the traditional communist governments, however, things began to happen that no one had predicted. The traditional communists that ran these countries were not really trusted by the people. In June 1989, free elections were held in Poland. This allowed people to vote for non-communists and the dramatic result was a non-communist government.

## Opening borders

During the Cold War, people could not freely move between eastern and western Europe. Borders were fenced and tightly controlled by armed guards. Germany itself was divided into a western half, friendly to the United States and western Europe, and an eastern half, friendly to the USSR. German people could not freely travel between the two halves of their own country, even though many people had friends and relatives living on the other side.

This map of Europe shows how Germany was divided into the Republic of West Germany, and the Soviet Zone until 1989.

Towards the end of 1989, the non-communist government that had emerged in Hungary made a dramatic announcement. Its borders with Austria, part of the West, would be thrown open. Up until then, people living in Soviet-controlled Eastern Europe could not freely travel to western Europe. Now they could.

East Germans had always been allowed to travel to Czechoslovakia and then Hungary. In the summer of 1989, they did so in the hope that Hungary would open its border with Austria. When this happened, they could drive across Austria and into West Germany.

This aerial view shows how the Berlin Wall divided the West (in the foreground) from the East (in the background), shown here in 1983.

## 1989: other news

**January**: George H. W. Bush succeeds Ronald Reagan as president of the United States, having defeated Michael Dukakis in the 1988 elections

**February**: investigators announce that the cause of the explosion on the Pan Am airplane that exploded over the Scottish town of Lockerbie was a bomb hidden inside a radio cassette player

**March**: in Egypt, a 4,400-year-old mummy is found in the Pyramid of Cheops

**April**: in Japan, Nintendo releases its popular Game Boy handheld video game player.

# Bringing down the Berlin Wall

## "Gorby, Gorby!"

Berlin, the capital of Germany, was situated in East Germany, but the city was split into two and divided by a wall. The Berlin Wall had been built by the East German government in 1961 to stop its citizens moving to the western half of the city, where they could gain access to West Germany and the rest of western Europe.

In October 1989, Gorbachev visited East Berlin and heard crowds of people chanting, "Gorby, Gorby, save us!" The following month saw millions of East Germans marching through the streets demanding an end to the closed borders. They wanted to move to West Germany, which did not have the economic problems that East Germany did. On 9 November, the government in East Berlin made an announcement that it hoped would help to slow down the rate at which people were leaving. A politician announced to journalists that East Germans could apply for a passport and visa and then travel freely to the West. "When? How soon?", asked journalists. The politician did not really know and replied, "It just means straight away." The news travelled fast.

That same night, 9 November 1989, East Berliners flocked to the Berlin Wall because they had heard the news. The guards were not sure what to do but one of them decided to open a gate in the wall and within a few hours people were streaming across into West Berlin. There was no violence.

East and West Germans start to tear down the Berlin Wall on 9 November 1989, after almost 30 years of division.

## The Wall comes down

By the morning of 10 November, bulldozers began pulling down a section of the wall to allow more people through. Pictures of what was happening were beamed around the world. By the evening, border guards from the East and West were swapping hats and people were arriving from other parts of Europe to celebrate.

Over the next few days, Berliners began to dismantle the wall for themselves and celebrations continued. People met relatives they had not seen for 28 years. Before the end of the month, West Germany was announcing its intention to unite East and West Germany.

## Problems ahead

Lots of East Germans were communists who, like Gorbachev, wanted a fairer society. They saw and admired the economy and freedom that West Germans were able to enjoy, and they also wanted free elections and a better standard of living. At the same time, they also saw less attractive aspects of life in western Europe, such as the enormous gap between the wealthy and the poor. They did not want to lose the benefits of their communist system, such as full employment, cheap housing, and free medical care. There would be problems creating one Germany out of two such different societies.

A young man uses a hammer and chisel to dismantle part of the Berlin Wall, November 1989.

## 9 November 1989: a night of drama

**6 p.m.** an East German politician announces that travel to the West would be possible for those with passports and visas

**9:30 p.m.** a guard, hearing the news on his radio, allows East Berliners (without passports or visas) to walk into West Berlin at the Bornholmer Strasse crossing

**10:30 p.m.** guards at other crossing points, hearing what was happening at Bornholmer Strasse, do the same

**11:59 p.m.** all the crossing points are opened and cars stream into West Berlin and join the midnight party that is taking place. Fireworks are lit and rockets blaze into the sky.

# Christmas in Romania

The changes that were sweeping across Eastern Europe were resisted by some of the traditional communist leaders. Erich Honecker, the East German leader, had wanted to use the army against demonstrators, but his own government overruled him.

## Romania

The leaders of Romania were more determined to resist change than any other government in Eastern Europe. President Ceaucescu and his family had ruled the country for over 20 years and they felt they could do what they liked. Ordinary Romanians feared Ceaucescu's secret police – the Securitate – because they killed people who were against the government.

## Revolution

The revolution began in mid December 1989 when a demonstration was held in the town of Timisoara in western Romania. Hundreds of the demonstrators were shot and killed by the security forces and this angered many people. Four days later, Ceaucescu and his wife appeared on the balcony of the headquarters of the Communist Party in Bucharest, the country's capital. His speech to the public was interrupted with boos and whistles from the crowd and the television cameras, under the control of the government, were switched off as the Ceaucescus hurriedly left the balcony.

Romanian President Nicolae Ceaucescu speaks from the balcony of the Communist Party headquarters during the revolution, 24 November 1989.

The streets of Bucharest became packed with citizens, angry about what had happened in Timisoara. Again, the security forces were ordered to open fire and many were killed. Large crowds gathered again the next day, but this time the security forces refused to shoot. The Ceaucescus tried to flee the country, but were arrested. After a short trial, they were shot by an execution squad on Christmas Day, 1989.

## Bulgaria and Albania

The leaders of Bulgaria and Albania saw what was happening to countries around them. They had a choice – to resist, as Ceaucescu had tried to do, or to allow free elections to take place. They chose not to resist. Bulgaria held elections in 1990 and the Bulgarian **Socialist** Party, made up of communists, formed a new government. In 1992, elections in Albania produced a non-communist government. Only in Yugoslavia did the end of communism lead to **civil war**. Opposing ethnic groups fought for control of the country and, despite many attempted peace negotiations, civil strife continued to dominate Yugoslavia throughout the 1990s.

Angry demonstrators in Timisoara, Romania, set fire to the flag of the Romanian Communist Party, 12 January 1990.

### An eyewitness

A Yugoslavian man was in Timisoara on the 18 December 1989 and witnessed what happened to the demonstrators:

"It was as if the whole city was on the street. Many of the demonstrators were students and schoolchildren but there were plenty of old people as well...Then I heard the sound of firing. It was the Securitate. They were shooting from helicopters in the air as well...One person saw two dead children being carried away in a white linen cloth."

The UK was also experiencing unrest as the 1980s drew to a close. The Conservative government had enjoyed power for a ten-year period of prosperity, but the economy was now in trouble. People were spending too much money, and **interest rates** increased sharply to try and slow down spending. Many people could no longer afford to pay their **mortgages** and so lost their houses. When the government introduced a new tax (nicknamed the poll tax) to replace the previous council tax there were large protests and a riot in London. The Prime Minister, Margaret Thatcher, was more unpopular than ever before.

## Change in China

The communist system in China, like that of the USSR, was badly in need of reform. The country's leader – Deng Xiaoping – set about reforming the economy. He introduced policies that were not unlike the perestroika ones of Gorbachev. Unlike Gorbachev, however, Deng Xiaoping had no intention of reforming the political system. He wanted to keep power strictly under control of the Communist Party.

Gorbachev visits Beijing where he is welcomed by the Chinese leader, Deng Xiaoping, on 16 May 1989. The visit marked an historic reconciliation between the two communist powers.

## Gorbachev visits Beijing

A visit to China's capital, Beijing, by Gorbachev was planned for May 1989. Chinese students wanted the kind of democracy that Gorbachev was introducing in the USSR. By the middle of April, students began gathering in the huge Tiananmen Square in the centre of Beijing. By the time of Gorbachev's visit, there were up to a quarter of a million student demonstrators in and around Tiananmen Square.

By the end of May, the Chinese government was faced with a problem. It knew what was happening in Eastern Europe and was worried that if it gave in to the students' demands, it might lose power altogether. The leaders who thought some democracy could be introduced without risking the collapse of the whole system were defeated. They lost their argument to those who decided the protests had to be crushed.

## Massacre in Tiananmen Square

On 3–4 June, the army moved against the students and opened fire using tanks and heavy weapons. It is not known how many were killed because the Chinese government only admitted 23 deaths. The total number was far higher than this, but estimates vary. Some say the number killed was 400 to 800, but others think it is more likely that as many as 1,500 to 3,000 were killed.

A student demonstrator bravely blocks the path of army tanks along the Avenue of Eternal Peace near Tiananmen Square, Beijing, China.

## Deng Xiaoping

Deng Xiaoping became the leader of China in 1977, after the death of Mao Zedong the year before. Xiaoping allowed industries to make their own decisions and reduced the power of the government over economic matters. He was not prepared to reduce the political power of the Communist Party, though. He died in 1997, but his policies have continued. They have made China very rich in economic terms and turned the country into a **superpower**.

# Change in South Africa

In South Africa, a system called **apartheid** had been created in the late 1940s. Apartheid allowed South Africa's minority population of white people to live a privileged life at the expense of the majority of the people, who were black (or Asian, or mixed race). In the countryside, black South Africans had to live in special reserves, and in the towns they were forced to live in special **townships** separated from the white areas. Racial **segregation** applied to transport, hospitals, sports, churches, and most aspects of social life. Whites wanted blacks to work in the mines, factories, and farms that made South Africa a wealthy country for the white minority. Black South Africans were paid badly, though, and they mostly lived in poverty.

## Opposing South Africa

By the 1970s, many were actively opposing apartheid. The biggest anti-apartheid organization, the **African National Congress (ANC)**, had its own **guerrilla army**. The United Nations voted to stop all trade with South Africa while apartheid lasted, but this did not work because lots of countries, including the UK and United States, carried on trading. They also sold weapons to South Africa because the Cold War was going on and South Africa supported the West and opposed communism in Africa.

By the 1980s, the South African economy was weak and governments in the West were advising it to make changes. In 1986, **Congress** stopped United States' loans and trade to South Africa, although President Reagan tried to stop this happening. Prime Minister Thatcher in the UK refused to do this, but was criticised by other countries. Around the world ordinary people opposed to the racism in South Africa continued to demonstrate. Many sporting organizations and musicians refused to play in South Africa.

Anti-apartheid demonstrators march with banners reading "Death to apartheid" in Boston, Massachusetts, United States, 1986.

## Making changes

By 1989, with the end of the Cold War in sight, the white leaders of South Africa knew they were internationally isolated. A new South African president – F. W. de Klerk – accepted that the black majority would have to be given equal rights, including the vote. He began to make important changes, hoping to make the best possible deal for the white minority.

All the remaining apartheid laws were removed and many black political prisoners were released from jail. This did not include Nelson Mandela, the head of the ANC, who had been in prison for 26 years but it was clear that he would have to be set free eventually.

### The Guildford Four

In the UK, in 1975, three men and one woman from Northern Ireland were convicted of the bombing of a pub in Guildford, Surrey, where five people were killed, and hundreds injured. Known as the Guildford Four, they claimed that they had been tortured by police to sign a confession. The Provisional IRA terrorist group later admitted that they were behind the attack. The Guildford Four were released in 1989, after being wrongly imprisoned for over a decade. It became accepted that the police had witheld important evidence to make the Four appear guilty.

Gerard Conlon, one of the Guildford Four, is released from prison after all of their convictions were found to be wrong, 19 October 1989.

The first year of the new decade, the 1990s, began with a number of interesting changes affecting the UK. Workers from France and the UK had been working beneath the English Channel building a road and rail tunnel. For a number of years they had worked towards each other from each side of the Channel. In 1990, they finally met, 40 metres (131 feet) below the sea. Just a week earlier, Margaret Thatcher, the Conservative prime minister since 1979, was forced to resign when she lost the support of her own party.

## 1990: A Year of Change

### Problems for Gorbachev

Gorbachev had not expected Communist governments in Eastern Europe to fall and for people to turn so eagerly to the Western way of running countries. Gorbachev had introduced democratic changes to the USSR, but he did not want to see the capitalist system being introduced – just some aspects of it that might strengthen the Soviet economy.

One problem was that the economic reforms set out in perestroika were not working. Prices began to rise and the standard of living was decreasing. Another problem was that some of the republics making up the USSR, seeing what was happening in Eastern Europe, began to demand their own independence. On top of these problems, Gorbachev was facing pressure from part of his own party. Some people thought he was in danger of breaking up the USSR and that the Communist Party would lose its influence.

Crowds of demonstrators, at a rally for independence, wave banners saying "Gorbachev! Go home!" Gorbachev was visiting Vilnius, Lithuania, in January 1990.

### Demanding independence

In January 1990, there was a massive demonstration of around 200,000 people in Lithuania, calling for independence from the USSR. Lithuania was in the western part of the USSR, by the Baltic Sea, and was one of the Baltic republics that had been taken over by the USSR during the Second World War. On March 11 1990, Lithuania declared itself independent, but the government of the USSR refused to accept this.

## Changes in 1990

- In Australia, after 150 years, *The Herald* newspaper was published for the last time. It was replaced by the *Herald-Sun*, a new paper that claimed to be the world's first 24-hour newspaper, with a morning and afternoon edition for each day.
- In Moscow, the first McDonalds restaurant opened.
- In South Africa, Nelson Mandela was released from prison, having spent 26 years behind bars for opposing the South African governments' racist policies.
- In Italy, the Leaning Tower of Pisa was closed to the public because safety experts thought it was in danger of falling over.
- In the United States, a number of film sequels were released including: *Die Hard 2*, *Back to the Future III*, *Rocky V* and *Predator 2*.
- In Ireland, Mary Robinson was elected as the first woman president of the country.

Nelson Mandela is led by his wife, Winnie, after his release from Victor Verster prison in Cape Town, South Africa, 11 February 1990.

# 1991: Drama in the USSR

At the start of 1991, in Vilnius – the capital of Lithuania – Soviet troops attacked the city's television broadcasting station and several people were killed. The television station had been broadcasting calls for Lithuanian independence and the attack was meant to frighten Lithuanians into remaining a part of the USSR.

Gorbachev said that he had not ordered the attack, but it is unclear who did. Gorbachev was also facing a challenge to his leadership from Boris Yeltsin, a politician who was standing for election as president of Russia, but not the whole of the USSR. Yeltsin was supporting the calls by the non-Russian republics of the USSR for more freedom.

## Gorbachev under arrest

Gorbachev tried to work with Yeltsin, and they agreed on plans to replace the USSR with a new union, so that both sides would be content. The Baltic republics – Lithuania, Latvia, and Estonia – along with Georgia, Armenia, and Moldavia (to become Moldova) would not be asked to join this union. Their claims to independence were more or less accepted.

There were, however, groups within the Communist Party who could not accept what was happening, and they decided to take their own action. They thought Gorbachev had betrayed the USSR by making huge changes to the traditional communist system. On 19 August 1991, Gorbachev was secretly arrested by these angry Communist groups. An Emergency Committee, which had taken power in Gorbachev's absence, announced he had resigned because of ill health. Gorbachev was not really ill, but the groups who felt he had betrayed the USSR wanted him removed from power.

## Dangerous times

Russian people were shocked by the news and did not know who or what to believe. The world was also shocked, and Western leaders wondered who now had control over the USSR's nuclear weapons.

The leaders behind the Emergency Committee sent tanks into the streets of Moscow. A crowd gathered and so did television crews. They witnessed a dramatic moment when Yeltsin came out from the Russian White House, wearing a bullet-proof vest under his suit, and climbed up on one of the tanks.

In an historic moment, Boris Yeltsin climbs up on to a military tank in the streets of Moscow and protests against Gorbachev's illegal arrest.

Yeltsin spoke to the public, and to the world, and said Gorbachev's arrest was illegal. The people responsible, he said, "must not be allowed to bring eternal night," meaning that Russia must stand up to these people.

## Gorbachev Released

Over the next few days the tension mounted in Moscow. Thousands of people took to the streets to demonstrate against the takeover. However, on the 21 August, the tanks withdrew from the centre of Moscow, and seven of the eight coup plotters were arrested (one committed suicide). Gorbachev was released, and briefly returned to power.

### A new map of the world

Yeltsin had become more popular than Gorbachev. There was now no stopping the break up of the USSR. A new Commonwealth of Independent States (CIS) was formed. It did not inlcude the Baltic republics, but did include a number of republics once part of the USSR, but now independent countries. On 25 December 1991, Gorbachev resigned and the USSR ceased to exist. Yeltsin became Russia's first democratically elected president.

The new countries of the CIS after the collapse of the USSR, Gorbachev, and communism, in 1991.

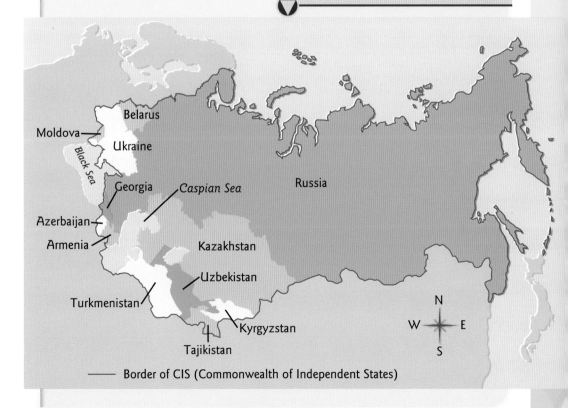

Border of CIS (Commonwealth of Independent States)

# The new Russia

*Kapitalizm*, Russian for capitalism, was introduced under Yeltsin in a series of sudden changes. Starting on the first day of 1992, most prices were no longer fixed by the government. They changed according to supply and demand and this system, called a **market economy**, saw most prices increase. The cost of a new car increased so much that the price of a car in January 1992 became the price for a spare tyre by the end of the same year.

A market economy allows people to buy and sell freely, and also to import and export goods without being controlled by the government. Public markets now began appearing in Russian towns. Economic advisers from the United States and western Europe were supporting Yeltsin, and they suggested further changes to the Russian way of life.

## Everything for sale

Under the old Soviet system, the government controlled most places of work. Everything was now to be sold and, to win the support of the people, every Russian received a voucher that could be used to buy a share in one of the new private companies. Worth about £15 at the time, the voucher could also be sold to anyone who could afford to buy it. Knowing they would increase in value, wealthy people and private companies began buying up the vouchers and, in the process, became very rich.

A market stall in Moscow sells imported fruit and vegetables after the old Soviet system is abandoned and a market economy is introduced.

## Shocking people

Many Russians found it very difficult to adjust to the system. Life was changing at a very fast pace. A lot of young people found it exciting and did not worry about the future or unemployment. Older citizens had more mixed feelings. Many agreed with Gorbachev when he argued that the communist system needed improving, but that it was worth keeping. They had believed that communism stood for fairness, but now understood that things needed to change. Said one Russian to a United States' journalist: "We lived for an idea. You Americans live just for money. We spent our whole lives working for an idea. Now it turns out you were right."

### A new generation gap

Older Russians, such as Vera Nikiferovna, found that her children had a different attitude towards life:

"I worked in a sewing factory for 41 years. I started when I was 14 years old. I got married young, lived with my husband, gave birth to children, raised them, and that's it. I don't have beautiful furniture. I don't have a beautiful apartment. I don't have a dacha [a holiday home in the country] or a car. I didn't earn anything in life. Now my children tell me I raised them the wrong way. All that honesty and fairness, no one needs it now. If you are honest you are a fool. They say we are going to live better but I don't know."

(FROM *KAPITALIZM* BY ROSE BRADY)

An elderly Russian woman carries loaves of bread in a Moscow market, November 1995.

# THE GULF WAR

The UK contributed 43,000 troops to the multinational force that went to war with Iraq in 1991. Before the war began in 1991, the Royal Navy was involved in helping to blockade the Persian Gulf, stopping any ships from reaching Iraq. This was to stop Iraq from exporting any oil or engaging in trade by sea. On 24 January, a few days after the first air strikes against Iraq began, a UK warship fired on three Iraqi ships. They had been operating from a small island belonging to Kuwait, but occupied by Iraq. Two Iraqi ships were sunk and, on the same day, UK and US forces captured the island. This was the first Kuwaiti **territory** to be freed.

Iraqi troops and their tanks roll into Kuwait City, Kuwait, on 2 August 1990.

## Background to the war

Iraq is made up of different ethnic and religious groups:

- a large **Kurdish** population in the north (the majority of whom are Sunni Muslim)
- Arab **Sunnis** in the centre of the country
- a **Shiite** population in the south.

The Sunni and Shiite are both followers of Islam. In 1979 there was a revolution in neighbouring Iran, and Shiite fundamentalists gained power. They believed that Arab societies should be run on strict religious lines and – their religion being Islam – they became known as Islamic fundamentalists.

## Iran-Iraq War

The Iranian Islamic fundamentalists called for an Islamic government in Iraq. They appealed to the Shiite population in the south of Iraq, and this increased the threat to Saddam Hussein – the leader of the non-Islamic Iraqi government, and a Sunni Muslim. To stop this threat, Iraq went to war with Iran in 1980.

## Iraq invades Kuwait

When the Iraq-Iran War ended in 1988, Iraq had debts of US$80 billion, which it had great difficulty in paying, and a declining standard of living. Saddam Hussein's problems would be solved if Iraq could gain some of the wealth of the oil-rich state of Kuwait.

Hussein asked Kuwait for a gift of US$30 billion and an annual payment of US$10 billion to help war-damaged Iraq. The war with Iran, Hussein argued, had saved Kuwait from Islamic fundamentalism. After Kuwait refused, Iraq invaded on 2 August 1990.

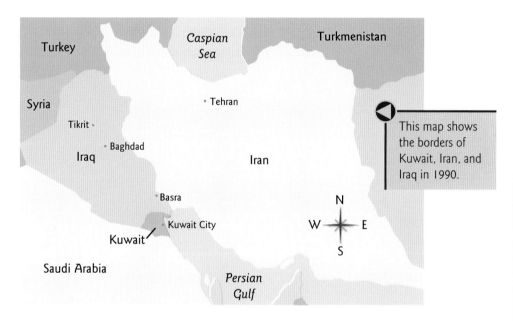

This map shows the borders of Kuwait, Iran, and Iraq in 1990.

## Saddam Hussein

Saddam Hussein was born in a village in the Tikrit district of Iraq in 1937 and moved to Baghdad at the age of ten. He joined the Ba'ath party in 1957, and helped it gain power and form a government in 1968. He was made a general in 1973 and by 1980 had secured control over the government. He was strongly supported by the Arab Sunnis, but less so by the Arab Shiites and the Kurds. He modernized Iraq, setting up free schooling and medical care, and did not allow religious groups to influence the government. He also became a harsh **dictator**, however, and anyone thought likely to oppose him was executed.

# Operation Desert Storm

## Resolution 660

Iraq's invasion of Kuwait was successful in that the Kuwaiti armed forces were defeated. However, the consequences were not what Saddam Hussein had planned. He had believed that the West would not interfere as long as the supply of oil from Kuwait was not stopped. He was mistaken about this. The West had large oil interests in Kuwait and Iraq's invasion was seen as a potential threat. On the day of the invasion, Resolution 660, calling on Iraq to immediately withdraw from Kuwait or face military force, was passed by the United Nations (UN).

The UN also refused to trade with Iraq and this cut off the export of oil from the country. The UN gave a deadline of 15 January 1991 for Iraq to withdraw from Kuwait, after which "all necessary means" would be used against Iraq. Hussein may have believed the UN would not really attack, or perhaps he felt that to back down would be a humiliating defeat. In any case, the deadline passed without Iraq withdrawing from Kuwait.

## A short war

On 16 January 1991, an international force launched Operation Desert Storm with the intention of removing Iraqi forces from Kuwait. The first stage of the operation was a series of bombing raids on military targets in Kuwait and Iraq, which lasted a month. This was followed, on 24 February, by a land attack against weakened Iraqi forces in Kuwait. Within three days, Kuwait City was recaptured and Hussein's army was driven back across the desert.

Iraqi women protest against the United Nations' sanctions forced on to Iraq. They wave an image of their leader, Saddam Hussein, outside the UN headquarters in Baghdad, Iraq.

## Consequences of the war

An estimated 200,000 Iraqis had died in the Gulf War by the time a **cease-fire** was agreed on 27 February. The United States decided not to capture Baghdad or remove Saddam Hussein from power. This was partly because Arab states – Egypt, Syria, Saudi Arabia, and Morocco – that had contributed troops to the UN force would not have agreed. Nor would France or the USSR have agreed. Also, the United States was worried about who would lead Iraq in place of Hussein – would, for example, the Islamic fundamentalists take control?

As a result of the Gulf War, there were uprisings against Hussein's government in the south and the north of Iraq. These uprisings did not receive any support from the West and were quickly defeated. Saddam Hussein's control over Iraq grew tighter.

### Chronology of Gulf War 1991:

| | |
|---|---|
| 12 January: | US Congress authorizes use of force |
| 17 January: | attack begins with an air force strike at 2:38 a.m. |
| 3 February: | first battleship gunfire against targets in Kuwait |
| 24 February: | attack begins |
| 26 February: | Iraqi forces begin fleeing Kuwait City |
| 27 February: | ceasefire agreed for 8 a.m. the following morning |
| 2 March: | US infantry troops attack fleeing Iraqi force, and untold numbers are killed. |

UN Marines line up in Hummer vehicles in the desert, during Operation Desert Storm, January 1991.

John Major, who had replaced Margaret Thatcher as prime minister in 1990, began to lose popularity. So did the Conservative government. There was a world **recession** and the economic prosperity of the 1980s was over. It seemed that people were willing to elect a Labour government. A general election took place in 1992 and most people expected Major to lose. The result was a surprise because Major was re-elected, although with a smaller majority of seats in **parliament**. The Labour Party looked for a new leader and eventually Tony Blair began to emerge as the favourite.

## The first intifada

The war between Iraq and Iran had dominated news about the Middle East for most of the 1980s. The position of the **Palestinians**, who were becoming angry because they felt that nothing was being done to help them, was largely forgotten about. Earlier wars between Israel and neighbouring Arab countries had resulted in many Palestinians living under Israeli rule, as well as in camps in Arab countries. By the late 1980s, Palestinians were still without their own country and the land that they lived on was called the Occupied Territories because it was controlled by Israel.

Beginning in December 1987, Palestinians in the Israeli-controlled land of the West Bank and Gaza Strip began a series of protests against the Israeli government. This became known as the *intifada* (uprising) and it lasted for 4 years. The *intifada* took the form of strikes, the non-payment of taxes, and demonstrations. It brought to the attention of the world the fact that Palestinians were angry at the way they were treated. The Israeli government used tough methods to try and put down the intifada and this was criticised by the United Nations.

Palestinian demonstrators wave the Palestinian flag and throw rocks during the *intifada* in the West Bank, Israel, February 1988.

## Seeking a Solution

The *intifada* was one of the reasons why the problem of Israel and the Palestinians came to world attention at the end of the 1980s and the early 1990s. Another reason was that the ending of the Cold War made it easier to seek a solution. The rivalry between the United States and the USSR was no longer making things more difficult.

The first talks between Israeli and Palestinian leaders took place in October 1991 in Madrid, Spain. Little progress was made until the following year when a general election took place in Israel. A new government, under Yitzhak Rabin, was formed. The prospects of some kind of settlement between Israel and the Palestinians became possible. The Palestinians wanted their own independent country, and Israel wanted to feel it was not going to be attacked by Arab groups.

## A new youth movement

In the north-west of the United States, especially around Seattle, a new kind of music was emerging. The lyrics told stories about real lives, and the followers of the music rejected the expensive designer clothes and shoes of mainstream pop culture. Bands such as Nirvana, Pearl Jam, Alice in Chains, and Soundgarden became very popular. Grunge clothing was a mixture of outdoors country clothing and the old punk styles, with torn jeans, checked shirts, and T-shirts. Eventually the music drew the attention of big recording companies and Grunge music, as it was called, was to become a strong influence in the United States and Europe.

The rock band Nirvana led the way, in both music and fashion, in the Grunge movement of the early 1990s.

# The break up of Yugoslavia

## An ethnic mix

The country called Yugoslavia was made up of six different states – Serbia, Croatia, Montenegro, Slovenia, Bosnia-Herzegovina, and Macedonia – with different mixes of nationalities and races living in many of them. In 1945, after the Second World War, Yugoslavia became a communist country and the different nationalities lived peacefully with one another. In 1980, divisions began to appear after the death of the communist leader, Tito.

Ethnic groups
- Serbs and Montenegrins
- Croats
- Muslims
- Slovenes
- Macedonians
- Albanians
- Hungarians
- Bulgarians
- Romanians, Slavs

This map shows the many ethnic divisions within Yugoslavia in 1991.

## Trouble in Serbia

In the 1980s, Yugoslavia's economy was suffering from unemployment and rapid increases in prices. In 1988 Slobodan Milosevic, a political leader in Serbia, began to stir up nationalist feelings in Serbia. Milosevic claimed that in Kosovo, a part of Serbia with a huge Albanian population, Serbians were being discriminated against by the Albanian majority. This increased his popularity and in 1990, when free elections were held in Serbia, he was this time elected as president of Serbia. He was not seen as a communist, but as a nationalist who promised to make Serbia the strongest country within Yugoslavia.

## Nationalism

The nationalism that began in Serbia spread to all parts of Yugoslavia. It was like a slow-working poison that, once released, created **ethnic** hatred and conflict. The UN was trying to keep the peace between Serbia and Croatia, but the two countries were not willing to reach a peaceful solution. By the end of 1991, Bosnia was threatening to break into civil war and, again, the UN was struggling to keep control. In September 1991, Macedonia declared its independence.

## Trouble in Croatia

Free elections were held in all the Yugoslav countries in 1990, and non-communist governments were elected in Croatia and Slovenia. They did not like what Milosevic was doing and began stirring up nationalist feelings about their own countries, against the threat of Serbian domination. In June 1991, Croatia and Slovenia declared themselves independent.

The problem was that over half a million Serbs lived in Croatia, making up about 15 per cent of the population. They were worried about what would happen to them in an independent Croatia. Serbia promised to help them. In June 1991, Serbian troops invaded the part of Croatia where many Serbs lived and by August they had captured a third of the country. The United Nations became involved and sent troops to keep a ceasefire that was agreed in August 1991. The Serbians had got hold of the parts of Croatia they wanted, so they were happy to accept a ceasefire.

French UN troops and their tanks roll into Croatia to ensure that the ceasefire is maintained, August 1991.

## Trouble in Bosnia

Just as the UN was trying to settle the conflict between Serbia and Croatia, trouble began to develop in Bosnia. There was a mixed population living in Bosnia, made up of 44 per cent Muslims, 33 per cent Serbs, and 17 per cent Croats. The Serbs in Bosnia were led by Radovan Karadzic and they wanted to remain with Serbia. The Muslims and Croats wanted their own independence. A chaotic and bloody war between the three groups began, lasting for over three years. The war finally ended with the Dayton Peace Agreement of November 1995, which divided the country of Bosnia between the rival groups.

# Unsolved problems

## Changing maps

By the end of 1991, the publishers of atlases were finding it difficult to keep up with the changing map of the world. The USSR had disappeared and many new countries had emerged. A united Germany was about to replace West Germany and East Germany. Yugoslavia was breaking up and nobody was too sure what the boundaries of the new independent countries would be.

## New and old conflicts

At the end of the Cold War people had hoped that a safer world would emerge, but the opposite was in danger of happening. Newly independent countries brought new conflicts to the surface and, in Yugoslavia, this was about to spill over into civil war. The war between Iraq and Iran had **destabilized** the Middle East and led to the Gulf War. Palestinians were asserting their right to be treated fairly. Only in South Africa did it look as if a peaceful solution might be found.

## Al-Qaeda

In 1988, an organization was formed called Al-Qaeda, although it did not attract a lot of attention at the time. It was formed by a very wealthy Saudi Arabian, Osama Bin Laden, and aimed to form an Islamic government in Afghanistan. It developed into a broader Islamic movement that was against the influence of the West in the Arab world. When the Gulf War broke out in 1991, Bin Laden had returned to Saudi Arabia and criticised his country for supporting what he saw as a war by the West against Islam. This led to him leaving Saudi Arabia for Sudan, where there was an Islamic government, and he continued to build up Al-Qaeda.

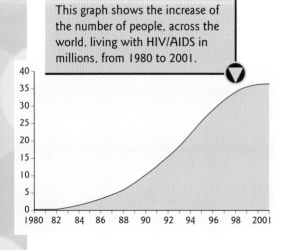

This graph shows the increase of the number of people, across the world, living with HIV/AIDS in millions, from 1980 to 2001.

## New epidemics

A new virus that forced itself into the news in the 1980s was human immunodeficiency virus (HIV). This virus seriously reduces the body's resistance to infection. It leads to a condition that can kill – called acquired immunodeficiency syndrome (AIDS). HIV was first identified in 1981, and by 1990 about 5 million people around the world were infected. This number would go on increasing because there remains no known cure. Although it has spread across the whole world, the number of HIV infections grew faster in southern Africa than anywhere else.

Some other diseases increased as a result of the lifestyle of people in the West. Between the mid 1980s and the early 1990s, more people began to die from smoking-related diseases and drinking alcohol. In Russia, where people found it difficult to adjust to the enormous changes taking place, there was a sharp increase in alcohol consumption.

## Compact discs to the Gulf War

The years between 1985 and 1991 began and ended with the following events:

1985:

- a joint US-French expedition located the wreck of the *Titanic*
- "New Coke" was released on the 99th anniversary of Coca-Cola, but it failed to sell and the original drink was brought back 2 months later
- US President Reagan sold the rights of his autobiography to a publisher for a record US$3 million.

1991:

- the second largest city in Russia, called Leningrad since 1924, was given back its old name of St Petersburg
- the US *Galileo* spacecraft becomes the first probe to approach an asteroid (called 951 Gaspra)
- Pan Am Airlines, the best-known United States airline, ended operations.

This is a moving AIDS awareness poster from the late 1980s.

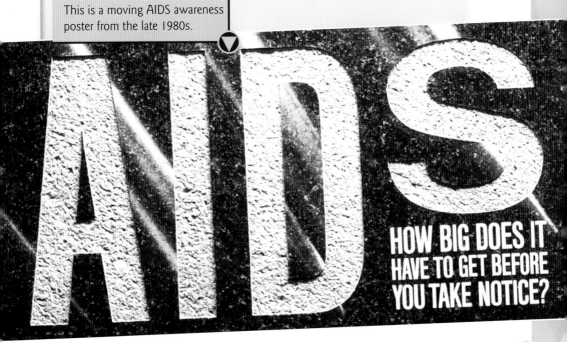

AIDS

HOW BIG DOES IT HAVE TO GET BEFORE YOU TAKE NOTICE?

# TIMELINE

## 1980-1983

First music CD players and discs are being sold

## 1985

Rap music becomes popular across the world

CD technology is adapted to computers

The Live Aid concert raises £150 million (US$245 million) for famine relief

TWA flight from Athens to Rome is hijacked

An Air India 747 is blown up over the west coast of Ireland

A cruise ship, the *Achille Lauro*, is hijacked in the Mediterranean

The *Rainbow Warrior* is blown up in Auckland, New Zealand

Mikhail Gorbachev is elected leader of the USSR

The wreck of the *Titanic* is found

## 1986

3 million CD players have been sold in the United States

Javits Convention Centre is opened in New York, United States

The first *Simpsons* cartoon is broadcast on Tracy Ullman's comedy show

France admits responsibility for the *Rainbow Warrior* explosion

Twenty-fifth anniversary of manned space flight

A space shuttle, the *Challenger*, explodes just after take-off, killing its seven crew members

A nuclear reactor at Chernobyl nuclear power plant in the Ukraine explodes, throwing clouds of radioactive gas into the atmosphere

## 1987

France pays Greenpeace US$8.16 million in compensation for the bombing of the *Rainbow Warrior*

The IRA plants a bomb in Enniskillen killing eleven people and injuring many more

The Palestinian *intifada* begins

## 1988

British troops kill three unarmed IRA members in Gibraltar

An earthquake in Armenia kills 50,000 people

A Pan Am flight from London to New York is blown up over Scotland

The war between Iran and Iraq ends

Al-Qaeda is formed

## 1989

Free elections are held in Poland

Hungary opens its borders with Austria

George H. W. Bush becomes president of the United States

A 4,400 year old mummy is found in the pyramid of Cheops, Egypt

Game Boy is released

The Berlin Wall is opened up for people to pass freely through

The dictator of Romania, Nicolae Ceaucescu, is deposed

Chinese troops open fire on protestors in Beijing

The system of apartheid is dismantled in South Africa

Four prisoners imprisoned for a pub bombing in Guilford are released and pardoned

## 1990

The sitcom *Seinfeld* is first shown

Bulgaria holds free elections

French and British engineers complete a tunnel under the English Channel

Lithuania declares itself independent of the USSR

The first McDonalds restaurant opens in Russia, in Moscow

Nelson Mandela is released from prison

Mary Robinson is elected the first woman president of the Republic of Ireland

Iraq invades Kuwait

## 1991

Soviet troops threaten the independence movement in Lithuania

An attempted coup in the USSR is prevented. Gorbachev resigns and the USSR is broken up

A multinational force invades Iraq

The first negotiations begin between the Palestinians and Israel aimed at an independent Palestinian homeland

Croatia and Slovenia declare independence from Yugoslavia

Serbian troops invade Croatia

Civil war begins in Bosnia

Leningrad in Russia changes its name back to St Petersburg

## 1992

Russia moves towards a capitalist economy

Elections are held in Albania

# FURTHER INFORMATION

## Books

*American Disasters: The Challenger Disaster*, Carmen Bredeson (Enslow, 1999)

*American Women at War: American Women of the Gulf War*, Heather Hasan (Rosen, 2004)

*Days that Changed the World: The Fall of the Berlin Wall*, Jeremy Smith (World Almanac, 2004)

*Disaster! Exxon Valdez: The Oil Spill off the Alaskan Coast*, Gil Chandler (Capstone, 2003)

*Fashion Sourcebooks: the 1980s*, John Peacock (Thames and Hudson, 1998)

*The Bombing of Pan Am Flight 103*, R. Dong Wicker (Rosen, 2003)

*20th Century Media: the 1990s: Electronic Media*, Steve Parker (Heinemann Library, 2001)

*20th Century Music: 80s & 90s: Different Paths*, Jackie Gaff (Heinemann Library, 2001)

*War and Conflict in the Middle East: The Gulf War*, Suzanne J. Murdico (Rosen, 2004)

*War and Conflict in the Middle East: The Six-Day War*, Matthew Broyles (Rosen, 2004)

## Websites

http://en.wikipedia.org/wiki/1900s
Encyclopedia with sections on the 1980s and 1990s.

http://geocities.com/historygateway/1900.html
Weblinks to interesting sites relevant to the history of women in the UK.

http://kclibrary.nhmccd.edu/decades.html
United States cultural history on a decade-by-decade basis.

## Disclaimer

All the internet addresses (URLs) given in this book were valid at the time of going to press. However, due to the dynamic nature of the Internet, some addresses may have changed, or sites may have ceased to exist since publication. While the author and publishers regret any inconvenience this may cause readers, no responsibility for any such changes can be accepted by either the author or the publishers.

## the mid **1980s** to the early **1990s**

| | |
|---|---|
| **Art and architecture** | • Vincent van Gogh's *Sunflowers* is sold for a massive $US39.9 million in 1987<br>• Thieves steal twelve works of art, including paintings by Degas, Rembrandt, and Renoir, valued at US$300 million, from a Boston museum. They have never been recovered. |
| **Books and literature** | • Audio books (books narrated on cassette tape or compact discs) become hugely popular<br>• The Nobel Prize for Literature is awarded to an African writer, Nigerian Wole Soyinka, in 1986, for the first time in history |
| **Education** | • Ruth Lawrence finishes her Oxford university degree in 1985. She is only thirteen years old. |
| **Fads and fashions** | • Cabbage Patch Kids, dolls that have a unique birth certificate and adoption papers, become instantly popular when they are introduced in 1983<br>• The Nintendo Game Boy is released with the game "Tetris." Three years after its release more than 32 million have been sold. |
| **Historic events** | • A terrorist bomb is detonated in the basement of the World Trade Center in New York, United States, 1993, killing 6 and injuring over 1,000<br>• The world's population passes the 5 billion (a thousand million) mark in 1990 |
| **People** | • Unseeded German tennis player, Boris Becker, wins the Wimbledon Tennis Championship, aged just seventeen |

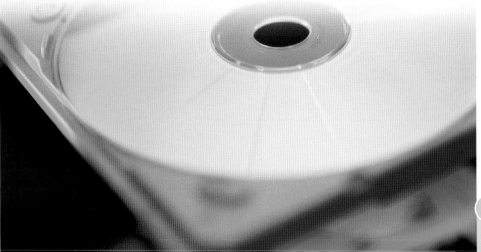

# GLOSSARY

**allied** on your side

**ANC** African National Congress, founded in 1912 as a liberation movement and banned between 1960 and 1990, now the governing party of South Africa

**apartheid** system of racial discrimination enforced in South Africa by white-only government until 1994

**binary code** way of showing information, using only 0 and 1, that computers can handle at a very fast rate

**capitalism** economic system based on private ownership and profit

**Catholic** group within the religion of Christianity

**cease-fire** agreement between opposing groups to stop shooting or fighting for a period of time

**civil war** war between groups within a country, not a war against another country

**civilian** non-military citizen

**Cold War** period of hostility that existed between the United States and the USSR between 1945 and the late 1980s

**communism** economic system based on government ownership and spreading wealth

**Congress** part of the law-making body of the United States

**democracy** government where people of the country choose their leaders by voting for them

**destabilize** to make unstable

**dictator** non-democratic ruler who controls the government

**economy** matters to do with money

**ethnic** to do with one race or cultural group

**evacuate** to depart in an organized way

**extremist** unwilling to compromise over a position that one regards as too one-sided

**famine** state of hunger affecting an entire community

**flotilla** group of ships

**fundamentalist** person who adopts an extreme position

**genetic** to do with inherited characteristics

**glasnost** a Russian word, which translates as "openness"

**guerrilla army** army fighting against government forces, but not engaging in an open battle

**interest rates** official rate at which money can be borrowed from a bank or a similar institution

**IRA** Irish Republican Army

**Islam** religion of Muslims

**Kurdish** to do with the Kurds, a people who live in parts of Iraq, Turkey, Iran, and Syria

**lacquer** hard varnish used to cover and protect the surface of a material

**loyalist** people and groups in Northern Ireland who wanted to remain a part of the UK

**Lycra** stretchy man-made fibre or fabric

**market economy** part of the capitalist economic system that allows prices to be determined by supply and demand

**masculine** having male qualities

**middle class** social group between the poor and the rich

**Middle East** mostly Arab countries located between Europe and Asia

**mortgage** loan of money for the purchase of a house

**Muslim** people who practise Islam

**mutated** change in the nature or shape of something

**nationalist** person with a strong belief in the value of their country

**nuclear reactor** part of a nuclear power station where nuclear particles undergo a controlled nuclear reaction to release energy

**Palestinian** person whose homeland is Israeli-controlled Palestine

**parliament** place where politicians make decisions and pass laws

**perestroika** Russian word meaning "to change the structure of something"

**PLO** Palestine Liberation Organization, developed out of the Israeli occupation of Palestinian territory and fought to establish an independent Palestine

**Protestant** Christian group

**radiation** release of rays of light and heat resulting from a nuclear explosion

**radioactive** something that gives off radiation, usually dangerous to humans

**recession** state of economic depression where people are buying less and unemployment is high

**Republican** people or groups in Ireland who want an end to British rule

**sanction** punitive action taken against a group or a country

**segregation** forcing racial groups to live separately in a community

**Shiite** member of the Shia religious group within Islam

**Sikh** member of the Sikh religious group within Islam

**socialist** someone who believes in a society that shares profit

**stalemate** position where neither side in a dispute can gain an outright victory

**suburb** area on the outskirts of a city

**Sunni** member of the Sunni religious group within Islam

**superpower** very powerful country with a lot of influence

**territory** land belonging to a particular group or country

**terrorist** person who uses violence and threats to try and force political change

**township** specially designated urban area where black people were forced to live in apartheid South Africa

**Unionist** member of the Unionist political party in Northern Ireland

**United Nations** international organization of countries. Its role is to maintain international peace, good relations, and security

**urban decay** urban area suffering from a lack of investment

**USSR** Union of Soviet Socialist Republics

**West** term referring to the way of life and government in Europe and North America

# INDEX

# Titles in the *Modern Eras Uncovered* series include:

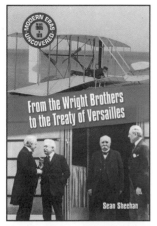

Hardback      1 844 43950 X

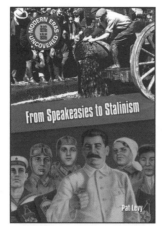

Hardback      1 844 43951 8

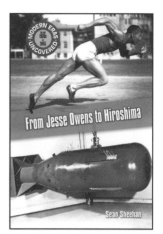

Hardback      1 844 43952 6

Hardback      1 844 43953 4

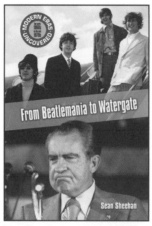

Hardback      1 844 43955 0

Hardback      1 844 43956 9

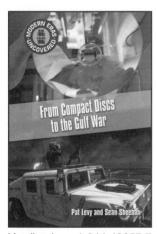

Hardback      1 844 43957 7

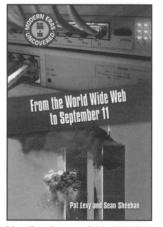

Hardback      1 844 43958 5

Find out about the other titles in this series on our website www.raintreepublishers.co.uk